STARGAZERS' GUIDES

What's Inside a Black Hole?

Deep Space Objects and Mysteries

Andrew Solway

Heinemann Library
Chicago, Illinois

Design by Richard Parker and Tinstar Design
Illustrations by Jeff Edwards
Printed in China by WKT Company Limited

10 09 08 07 06
10 9 8 7 6 5 4 3 2 1

Library of Congress Cataloging-in-Publication Data
Solway, Andrew.
 What's inside a black hole? : deep space objects and mysteries / Andrew Solway.
    p. cm. -- (Stargazers guides)
 Includes bibliographical references and index.
 ISBN 1-4034-7710-8 (library binding - hardcover) -- ISBN 1-4034-7717-5 (pbk.)
 1. Cosmology--Juvenile literature. 2. Astronomy--Juvenile literature. 3. Stars--Juvenile literature. 4. Interstellar matter--Juvenile literature. 5. Black holes (Astronomy)--Juvenile literature. I. Title. II. Series.
 QB983.S72 2006
 523.1--dc22
                              2005029113

Acknowledgments
The author and publishers are grateful to the following for permission to reproduce copyright material: Galaxy pp. **4** (David Cortner), **9** (Robin Scagell), **11** (Robin Scagell), **19** (Ian Morrison), **20** (Y Hirose), **28** (Todd Boroson/Noao/Aura/Nsf), **29** (Robin Scagell), **30** left (Noao/Aura/Nsf), **31** (Stsci/Aura), **33** (Stsci), **34** (Nuffield Radio Astronomy Observatory), **40** (Stsci), **41** (Kamioka Observatory/Icrr/University Of Tokyo); Getty Images p. **27** (Photodisc); NASA Headquarters - Greatest Images Of NASA pp. **10**, **30** right; Paramount Television p. **25** (Ronald Grant Archives); Science Photo Library pp. **5** (Jerry Lodriguss), **8** (Frank Zullo), **13** (Luke Dodd), **14**, **15** (Mpia-Hd, Birkle, Slawik), **16** (Efda-Jet), **18** (European Southern Observatory), **21** (David A. Hardy, Futures: 50 Years In Space), **23** (US Library Of Congress), **24** (Mark Garlick), **26**, **32** left (Chandra X-Ray Observatory/NASA), **32** right (Canada-France-Hawaii Telescope/Jean-Charles Cuillandre), **35** (Lynette Cook), **36** (Noao), **37** (Emilio Segre Visual Archives/American Institute Of Physics), **38** (Mark Garlick), **42**, **43** (Mehau Kulyk); Science Photo Library/NASA pp. **17**, **39**.

Cover image of a black hole reproduced with permission of the Science Photo Library.

The publishers would like to thank Dr. Geza Gyuk of the Adler Planetarium in Chicago for his assistance in the preparation of this book.

Every effort has been made to contact copyright holders of any material reproduced in this book. Any omissions will be rectified in subsequent printings if notice is given to the publishers. The paper used to print this book comes from sustainable resources.

Disclaimer
All the Internet addresses (URLs) given in this book were valid at the time of going to press. However, due to the dynamic nature of the Internet, some addresses may have changed, or sites may have ceased to exist since publication. While the author and publishers regret any inconvenience this may cause readers, no responsibility for any such changes can be accepted by either the author or the publishers.

Contents

Words appearing in the text in bold, **like this**, are explained in the Glossary.

The Universe in the Sky

Next time there is a dark, clear night, take a good look at the sky. What do you see? The blackness of the night is peppered with thousands of tiny lights. At first they all look the same: they all are just stars. But as you look more carefully, you start to see differences. The stars are not evenly spread—there are groups and patterns. Some stars are brighter than others. Some of them are not points of light, but rather are fuzzy patches. If you look carefully, you will see that they are not all the same color, either.

Astronomers know much more about the night sky than they did 100 years ago. They have been helped by powerful telescopes and computers.

HOW IT WORKS:

Twinkle, little star . . .

Stars do not seem to be steady points of light. They twinkle, as if they are winking on and off. If you could fly into space, you would see that, in fact, most stars produce a steady light. The twinkling happens because the **atmosphere**—the layer of air that blankets Earth's surface—varies. Some of it is moving, and in some places the air is **denser** (thicker) than in others. These differences in the air affect the light coming from the stars, making them seem to flicker.

Seeing the universe

When you look at the night sky, you are actually looking beyond our small corner of space into the vast distances of the **universe**. The stars that twinkle in the night sky are incredibly far away from us. The fuzzy patches may not be stars at all. They could be enormous clouds of gas or light from another **galaxy** that is far, far beyond our own.

Amazing discoveries

Over the past 100 years, astronomers have made incredible discoveries about the universe we see in the night sky. They have learned that the universe is much, much bigger than we ever imagined. They have found exploding stars and galaxies crashing into each other. And they have found evidence of **black holes**—areas of space that suck in everything around them, even light.

But what's inside a black hole? You can find that out later in this book.

There is plenty to see in the night sky with just the naked eye. With a telescope, or even a pair of powerful binoculars, you can see much more.

Shapes in the Sky

Stars are not evenly sprinkled across the night sky. Some stars are brighter than others. In some places the stars are grouped closely together, while in other places they are far apart. If you look carefully, you will begin to find patterns that you can remember.

Constellations

People have been finding patterns in the stars for thousands of years. Patterns of this kind are called **constellations**.

Without the constellations, all you see is a jumble of bright points. But once you begin to recognize constellations, they help you make sense of the night sky. You notice differences in the positions of the stars from one night to another.

The stars in a constellation are not really grouped together. We only see them that way from Earth. The table below shows how far away from Earth each of the stars in Orion really is.

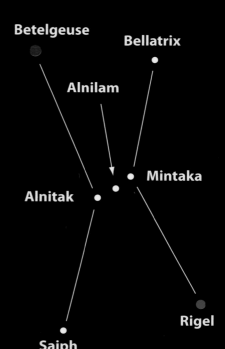

Star name	Part of Orion	Approximate distance from Earth (light-years)
Betelgeuse	left shoulder	600
Bellatrix	right shoulder	450
Alnitak	left belt	1,500
Alnilam	center belt	1,500
Mintaka	right belt	1,500
Saiph	left foot	720
Rigel	right foot	900

Estimates of the distances to stars vary a lot in different sources.
These figures are from the NRAO (National Radio Astronomy Observatory).

People in different parts of the world and at different times in history have found different constellations in the sky. Today, astronomers around the world divide the sky into 88 different constellations. At the equator, you can see all the constellations. However, as you go north or south from the equator, some constellations drop below the horizon. So, for example, in northern parts of the world, it is not possible to see the Southern Cross.

TRY IT YOURSELF:
Find a constellation

In the southern hemisphere, Centaurus is the most impressive constellation. You can find it by looking for the very bright stars Alpha Centauri and Beta Centauri, which are the centaur's two front feet. Between the "legs" of the centaur is another famous constellation, Crux.

From August to September, the constellation of Orion is one of the most obvious in northern skies. But the best time to look for Orion is in December, when it is high in the sky. Look for the three stars of Orion's belt. They are one of the easiest groups of stars to spot. From there, you should be able to spot the rest of Orion.

These are some of the main constellations you might see in December in the northern hemisphere. Many of them lie along a line called the ecliptic. The ecliptic is the path of the Sun through the day.

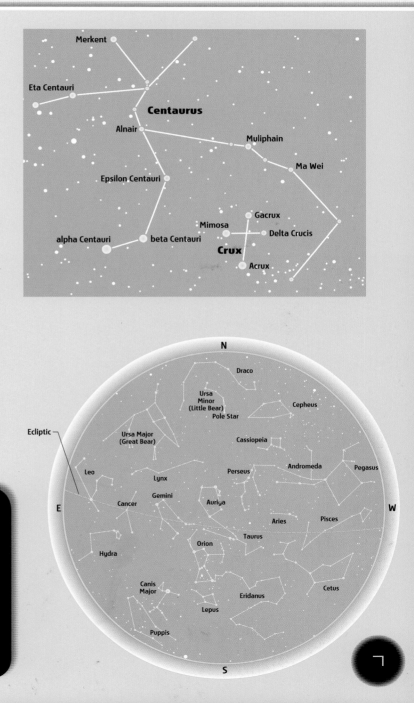

7

The Changing Sky

It takes time to spot constellations, because they do not stay still. They move across the sky during the night. The constellations you can see also change slowly over the course of the year. All these changes mean that, unless you are very experienced, you can never be sure where to look for a constellation. However, some constellations, such as Orion, are quite easy to spot with a little practice. You can also get books and star maps to help you.

Circling in the night

Stars move across the sky through the night. In the northern hemisphere, they circle the pole star, which hardly seems to move. In the southern hemisphere, the stars also circle, but there is no star at the central point.

To us on Earth, it seems as if the stars are moving across the sky. In fact, it is Earth that is moving, while the stars stay still. As Earth turns on its **axis**, the stars seem to circle in the sky.

By keeping the shutter of a camera open for the whole night, we can take a picture like this. It shows how stars appear to move in a circle during the night.

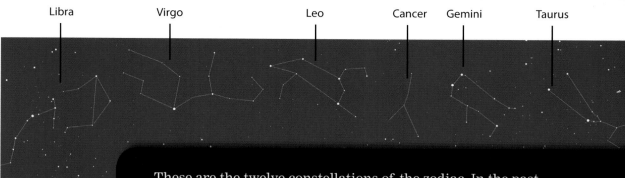

Libra   Virgo   Leo   Cancer   Gemini   Taurus

These are the twelve constellations of the zodiac. In the past, world leaders checked with an astrologer to make sure the stars were in their favor before they began any important task.

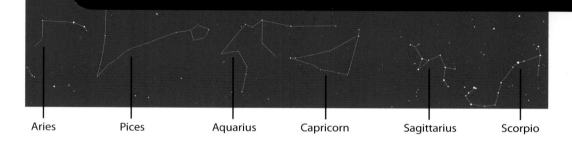

Aries   Pices   Aquarius   Capricorn   Sagittarius   Scorpio

HOW IT WORKS:

The zodiac

The zodiac is a group of twelve constellations that appear in the northern hemisphere at different times of year. In the past, some people used these constellations as a sort of calendar. Each constellation appears above the horizon at the same time every year.

The zodiac constellations are also part of **astrology**, or reading your future in the stars. In astrology, each of the twelve zodiac constellations is a star sign. Everyone has a particular star sign, depending on when they were born. For instance, if you were born between March 21 and April 19, your star sign is Aries (the Ram), because of the position of Aries in the sky at this time. Astrologers believe they can make predictions about what might happen to you in the future based on what is happening to your star sign in the sky. However, there is no scientific proof that astrology works.

Changing with the seasons

The stars also change with the seasons. For instance, in the northern hemisphere, Orion is visible from August to May. The changes happen because the parts of the sky we can see change as Earth **orbits** (goes around) the Sun. At any one time, our view of some stars is blocked by the Sun.

9

Looking into the Past

Every one of the thousands of stars we can see from Earth is a huge, hot ball of gas. Our Sun is a star, too, but it is much closer than the other stars. It is so close that we can feel its heat and so bright that we should not look at it directly.

The stars in the night sky are small and dim because they are incredibly far away from us. The fastest that astronauts have ever traveled is about 25,000 mph (40,000 km/h). Traveling at this speed, it would take 90,000 years to reach even the closest star!

Speed of light

Measuring the distance from Earth to a star in miles or kilometers is a bit like measuring the distance from New York to London in inches or millimeters. The unit of measurement is just too small. So, astronomers measure distances between stars in **light-years**. Light travels very, very fast. A light beam can travel 186,000 miles (300,000 kilometers) in just one second. Light can travel to the Moon and back in 2.5 seconds, and light takes just 8.3 minutes to get from the Sun to Earth. A light-year is the distance light travels in one year—nearly 6 trillion miles (10 trillion kilometers)! The closest star to us (Proxima Centauri in the constellation Centaurus) is over four light-years away.

This picture shows Earth as seen from the Moon. Light takes about 1.25 seconds to travel from the Moon to Earth.

Seeing the past

When we look at the stars, we are doing something very strange: we are looking back in time. The star Rigel, for instance, which is part of the Orion constellation, is about 900 light-years from Earth. When we see Rigel in the sky, we are seeing light that left the star 900 years ago.

If the star Rigel (center) exploded today, we would not know about it until 2500. This is because light from Rigel takes so long to reach us.

TRY IT YOURSELF:
Look back in time

The next dark, clear night, go outside and find a star you can identify (perhaps one of the stars in Orion or Centaurus). Look the star up on the Internet and find out how far away it is. How many years ago did the light leave the star? What was happening on Earth at that time?

Types of Star

All stars are similar in many ways to the Sun. However, there are big differences in the size and temperature of different stars.

Red dwarfs

In general, the bigger a star is, the hotter it gets and the brighter it shines. The most common stars are **red dwarfs**, which are smaller than the Sun and shine less brightly. They are red because the surface is not very hot for a star—about 5,400 °F (3,000 °C). The star Alpha Centauri in the Centaurus system is actually made up of three stars close together. The smallest of them is a red dwarf called Proxima Centauri. It is the closest star to our Sun. Our Sun is a fairly small star, a yellow dwarf.

The red dwarf Proxima Centauri is less than one-tenth the size of the Sun and shines 10,000 times less brightly. The supergiant Rigel is 70 times larger than the Sun and 66,000 times brighter. Betelgeuse is even bigger than Rigel, but shines less brightly.

Yellow
dwarf
(our Sun)

Blue supergiant
(Rigel)

Red
dwarf
(Proxima
Centauri)

Red supergiant
(Betelgeuse)

Supergiants

The largest stars are called **supergiants**. They are much bigger than the Sun and shine far more brightly. Young supergiant stars are very hot—over 45,000 °F (25,000 °C)—and they shine with a bluish light. The star Rigel is one of these.

Big but cool

Some stars do not fit the general rule that big stars are hotter than small ones. The star Betelgeuse in the Orion constellation is a red supergiant. It is bigger than Rigel, but it is not much hotter than a red dwarf. This is because Betelgeuse is an old star.

Stars do not last forever. For millions or billions of years, they shine unchanged. But eventually they get old, like Betelgeuse, and then go out. Depending on their size, stars go out in a puff of gas—or with a huge bang!

This photograph was taken using a telescope. It shows stars of different sizes and colors. How many colors can you see?

A Star Is Born

The stars in the sky never seem to change. The constellations we see in the sky have been there since the start of human history. Yet stars are not everlasting.

Stars are born from huge clouds of gas, and they shine for many years. The gas they are made from is the fuel that keeps them shining. A supergiant burns through its fuel in a few million years. A yellow dwarf, like our Sun, can last five to ten billion years. A red dwarf shines for 100 billion years or more. Yet eventually even a red dwarf runs out of fuel, and its life ends.

Born from gravity

Stars produce their heat by **nuclear reactions** (see pages 16–17). However, the force that starts off these nuclear reactions is **gravity**. Gravity is a force that pulls everything in the universe toward everything else. The more massive (heavy) an object is, the stronger its pull.

In this picture, stars are forming in a huge gas cloud in the Orion Nebula.

Stars start life as a huge cloud of gas spread out in space. The force of gravity gradually pulls the gas together. As the gas cloud gets more dense (thicker), its gravity gets stronger. The gas at the center of the cloud begins to get crushed.

Crushing, or compressing, a gas makes it hotter. As gravity compresses the gas, the gas cloud begins to heat up. Eventually it gets hot enough for nuclear reactions to start, and then stars are born.

TRY IT YOURSELF:
Compress a gas

You can see how compressing a gas heats it up if you pump up a bike tire. Pump until the tire is as hard as you can make it. Then, feel the bottom of the pump (be careful not to touch any metal parts of the pump). You will find that it has become quite warm.

The Pleiades are a group of hot, blue stars that formed together about 100 million years ago.

Ten Billion Years of Sunshine

Stars produce incredible amounts of energy. Our Sun is only a smallish star. Yet every second, it produces as much energy as two billion of the world's largest power plants generate in a year! How do stars do it? Scientists have learned a lot about how stars shine by looking at our nearest star, the Sun.

Nuclear fusion

The Sun and other stars are made mostly from the gas **hydrogen**. They get their energy from a process called **nuclear fusion** (fusion means "joining together"). During nuclear fusion, hydrogen **atoms** join together to form atoms of another gas, called helium. This reaction produces an enormous amount of energy.

The nuclear power stations that produce some of our electricity work by using nuclear reactions. However, they use a different kind of reaction, which produces far less energy.

This is the inside of an experimental fusion reactor.

HOT NEWS:
Star power

Scientists are trying to find ways of getting energy from nuclear fusion on Earth. At the moment, their experiments use almost as much energy as they produce. However, in the future, fusion might give us almost unlimited supplies of energy.

The end of the Sun?

The Sun contains huge amounts of hydrogen fuel, but eventually most of it will be converted into helium. When this happens, the Sun will cool down a little and turn red. It will also swell enormously. The swelling Sun may get so big that it swallows Earth. Even if it does not, Earth will be too hot for living creatures to survive.

After some time as a giant red star, the outer layers of gas will blow off, and the rest of the Sun will collapse in on itself. The result will be a tiny, hot, heavy star called a **white dwarf**, which will slowly cool down.

All this will happen, but not for a long time. It will be another five billion years before the Sun starts to run out of fuel.

The Sun is like a huge, bubbling cauldron. The surface is always swirling and moving. Some areas are much hotter than others, and in some places huge flames jet out into space.

Exploding Stars

A large star shines for only a few million years before all its fuel is used up. Like a smaller star, it then swells up to become a huge supergiant. It may shine like this for another 100,000 years or more. Then, it dies in an incredible explosion called a **supernova**.

Supernova

A supernova happens very quickly. In less than a second, gravity crushes the center of the star into a small ball of incredibly dense material. This powerful crushing of the star's gases also produces huge amounts of heat. The outer parts of the star are blown into space in an incredible explosion, which can last several weeks. During this time, the star may shine billions of times more brightly than normal.

This picture shows a huge gas cloud called the Crab Nebula. It is the remains of a supernova that Chinese astronomers watched in 1054.

After the explosion

After a supernova, all that is left is the tiny, incredibly heavy ball that formed at the start of the explosion. This is called a **neutron star**. A neutron star is only about 6.2 miles (10 kilometers) across, but it is more massive (weighs more) than the Sun.

When a neutron star first forms, it is spinning very fast. This is because the spin of the star speeds up as the star collapses and becomes smaller, in the same way that ice skaters spin faster when they pull in their arms. The neutron star sends out very powerful beams of energy as it spins. These beams spread out into space like the beams of a cosmic lighthouse.

SCIENCE FACT OR SCIENCE FICTION: Alien signals?

In 1967 Jocelyn Bell-Burnell was using a **radio telescope** to scan large areas of space. One night she picked up a signal that went on and on in a regular pulse. What was it? Soon other scientists picked up the pulse, too. Some people thought it was a signal from aliens. They called it LGM, which stood for "Little Green Men." But Bell-Burnell found the real explanation: it was a beam of energy from a pulsar, a rotating neutron star.

A radio telescope can "see" objects in space such as neutron stars, which do not produce light but give out radio waves.

Black Holes and Wormholes

Supernovas and neutron stars are not the end of the story. When a really massive star explodes, the middle of the star collapses into a tiny speck of **matter**. However, this speck is heavier than the Sun!

The pull of gravity from something so small and heavy is incredibly strong. Nothing can escape from this pull, not even rays of light. It is like a hole in space—a black hole.

The Cygnus X-1 black hole is in the constellation Cygnus (the Swan). It is about halfway down the swan's "neck." The partner star can only be seen with a very powerful telescope, because it is 14,000 light-years from Earth.

Cygnus
X-1

HOT NEWS:
Seeing black holes

If a black hole is black, how can we ever see one? In 1971 astronomers discovered something unusual in the constellation Cygnus (the Swan). A huge blue star was going around and around another object that was invisible. Measurements showed that the invisible object was very heavy. It was almost certainly a black hole.

The black hole pulls gas off the blue (partner) star. As it falls toward the black hole, this gas gets extremely hot and glows. Although the black hole itself is not visible, there is bright ring of gas around it that can be seen.

The event horizon

It might seem that something with such strong gravity as a black hole would suck in everything around it. But, in fact, this doesn't happen. The outer surface of a black hole is not the actual solid material that the black hole is made of. That material is just a tiny speck at the center of the hole. The outer surface is something called the **event horizon**. Anything that gets this close to a black hole cannot escape and is pulled into it.

So, how big is the event horizon? That depends on the **mass** (weight) of the black hole. A black hole that forms when a huge star explodes has a mass about ten times more than our Sun. For a black hole of this mass, the event horizon is only about 18.6 miles (30 kilometers) across. Beyond this point, the gravity of the black hole is not strong enough to stop light from escaping. For more massive black holes, the event horizon is bigger.

This picture shows how Cygnus X-1 and its partner star might look.

What's Inside a Black Hole?

Scientists think they have quite a good idea of what a black hole is like. In order to understand their idea, it helps to imagine that you are falling into a black hole, feet first.

Going inside

As you move toward the black hole, you get pulled faster and faster. You also begin to feel stretched. This is because your feet are closer to the black hole than to your head. So, the pull of the black hole's gravity is stronger on your feet than on your head.

When you cross the event horizon . . . nothing happens! The stretching continues, but you can still see the outside world. Light can get into the black hole—it just can't get out. Yet as you get closer to the center of the black hole, you are stretched so much that you are pulled apart. Ouch!

The gravity of a planet such as Earth bends space and time just a little. A star bends it more, but a black hole makes a deep hole in space and time.

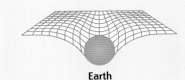

Earth

Star

Black hole

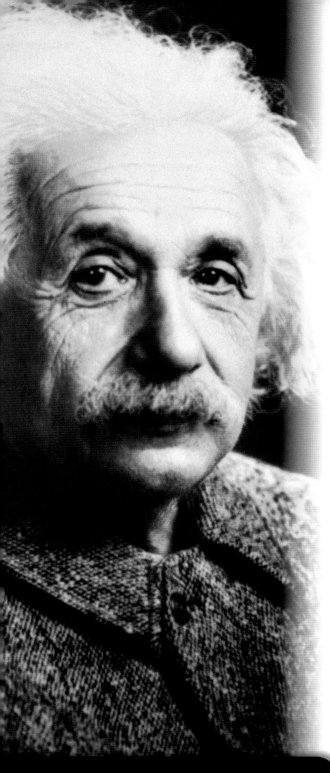

Watching from outside

If someone is watching as you go into the black hole, what they see is very different. As you get closer to the event horizon, you seem to slow down rather than speed up. As you reach the event horizon, you seem to stop moving altogether!

Although the watcher seems to see you slow down, what is actually slowing down is the light coming from you. As you get closer to the event horizon, light is slowed down by the gravity of the black hole, and it takes longer to reach the person watching. Gravity also has an effect on time itself. According to the famous scientist Albert Einstein, gravity slows time down!

HOT NEWS:
Everything is relative

Albert Einstein figured out his general theory of relativity in 1916. He discovered that gravity changes space and time. The stronger the gravity of an object, the more effect it has on space and time. One way to imagine this is to think of space and time as a sheet of stretched rubber. A light object will make a small dent in the rubber. A small, heavy object will make a very deep dent. Scientists think that a black hole makes a very deep hole in space and time.

Albert Einstein's theory of relativity is important because it helps to predict what happens around black holes.

Black Holes and White Holes

There is strong evidence that black holes really do exist. Yet there are even stranger possibilities than black holes. Albert Einstein and another scientist, Nathan Rosen, showed in 1935 that a black hole could have two "ends," not just one. They called this double-ended black hole an Einstein–Rosen bridge. Today, it is known as a wormhole.

In theory, a wormhole is a connection between two places in ordinary space. At one end of the wormhole there is a black hole, which connects to a "white hole"—a hole in space that throws out material in the same way that a black hole sucks it in. A wormhole could connect two areas of space that are close together, or areas that are far apart. It could even connect our universe with another, completely different one.

So, if a wormhole could be found or even made, it could perhaps be a way to travel very quickly from one place to another. However, there are problems with this idea. According to the theory that Einstein and Rosen figured out, wormholes are unstable. They only exist for a fraction of a second, before they "break" in the middle to form two separate black holes.

A wormhole connects two areas of space and time. Unfortunately, the connection stays open for only a very short length of time.

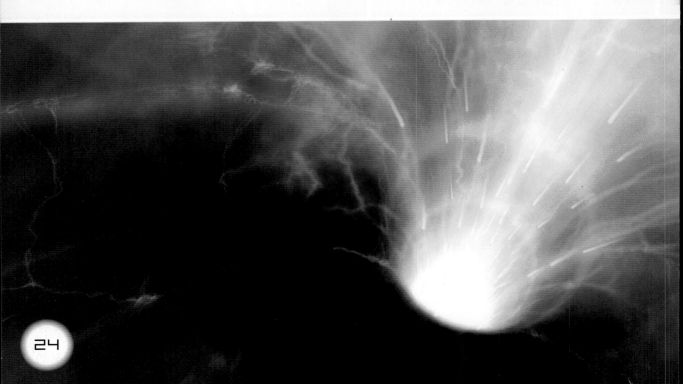

Since scientists first suggested that wormholes could connect different areas of space, writers and filmmakers have been using the idea in science fiction stories. Spaceships in *Star Trek* (above) often use wormholes to travel across the universe.

Unlimited travel?

Some scientists think that the problems of traveling through wormholes could be solved eventually. If they were, it might be possible to make a wormhole between, say, Earth and the star Rigel, 900 light-years away. Light from Rigel takes 900 years to reach Earth, but using a wormhole, it should be possible to travel there in a few moments. It might even be possible to travel through a wormhole into an entirely different universe.

SCIENCE FACT OR SCIENCE FICTION?

In 1985 the astronomer Carl Sagan wrote a science fiction book called *Contact*. In the book, a group of people travel all around the universe using wormholes. Although the story was fiction, Carl Sagan built the book around real science. Physics students at the California Institute of Technology had figured out that traveling in this way was possible in theory, although it is far beyond human abilities at the moment.

Gas and Dust

Clouds of gas and dust play an important part in the lives of stars. New stars form in large clouds of gas. Also, when a star ends its life, part of it becomes gas and dust.

Little clouds

Even before astronomers had powerful telescopes, they were able to see that some "stars" were not points of light. They were more like tiny clouds. Astronomers called them **nebulas** ("nebula" is the Latin word for cloud).

With powerful telescopes, astronomers can now look more closely at these nebulas. Many of them are beautiful, multicolored gas clouds. Some areas are bright, because they are lit by stars, or because the gases are hot enough to produce their own light. Other areas are dark, because clouds of dust block the light.

"Star nurseries" like this are huge clouds of gas and dust where new stars are born.

When our Sun eventually dies, it will form a planetary nebula similar to this one, the Cat's Eye Nebula.

Different types

Nebulas can form in different ways and vary in size. Some enormous patches of gas gather gradually over millions of years. Parts of these huge clouds are star nurseries, where new stars are forming. The Orion nebula, in the constellation Orion, and the Carina nebula, close to the Southern Cross, are both nebulas of this kind.

Other nebulas are produced by dying stars. Planetary nebulas are rings of gas and dust blown off by small to medium stars as they collapse and form white dwarfs. Nebulas, such as the Crab Nebula (see page 18), are the remains of supernova explosions.

Biography:
William Herschel (1738–1822)

William Herschel was born in Germany, but lived most of his life in England. Most astronomers of Herschel's time studied the Sun, the Moon, and the planets, because these were the only objects within range of their telescopes. But Herschel had different ideas. He studied telescope building and built some of the biggest telescopes in the world at the time. With the help of his sister Caroline and his son John, he carefully described several thousand different nebulas and other objects in the sky.

Galaxies

Not all the "fuzzy stars" that early astronomers called nebulas have turned out to be gas clouds. Some are tightly packed groups of stars known as star clusters. Others are huge "star islands" containing millions or billions of stars. These are known as galaxies.

Our galaxy

The Sun and Earth are part of a huge galaxy called the **Milky Way**. This galaxy is about 100,000 light-years across and contains around 100 billion stars. It is shaped like a flat disc, with a bulge at the center. This area is full of older stars. The whole Milky Way turns around the center.

Spiraling out from the central bulge are several arms. These spiral arms are a mixture of stars, gas, and dust. New stars are constantly being created here.

We cannot see the spiral shape of the Milky Way because we are part of it. However, we can see other spiral galaxies similar to ours, like this one.

HOT NEWS:
Massive black hole!

At the center of our galaxy, there is a massive black hole that weighs as much as 3.5 million Suns. The event horizon is about 14 million miles (22 million kilometers) across. This black hole was first discovered in 1974, but it is hard to see because it is hidden by a fog of dust.

The Andromeda galaxy

The Milky Way is only one of the billions of galaxies in the universe. The closest large galaxy to ours is the Andromeda galaxy. This is another spiral galaxy, even larger than the Milky Way. It is over 200,000 light-years across.

Although Andromeda is close as galaxies go, it is still incredibly far away from us. The light that we see coming from Andromeda left the galaxy two million years ago!

TRY IT YOURSELF:
See another galaxy

On a dark night, you may be able to see Andromeda as a faint blur in the sky, but it is easier to see with a pair of binoculars. To find Andromeda, first look for the W shape of Cassiopeia. Close to this is the great square of Pegasus. On one corner of Pegasus is the Andromeda constellation. The Andromeda galaxy is close to the middle of the constellation.

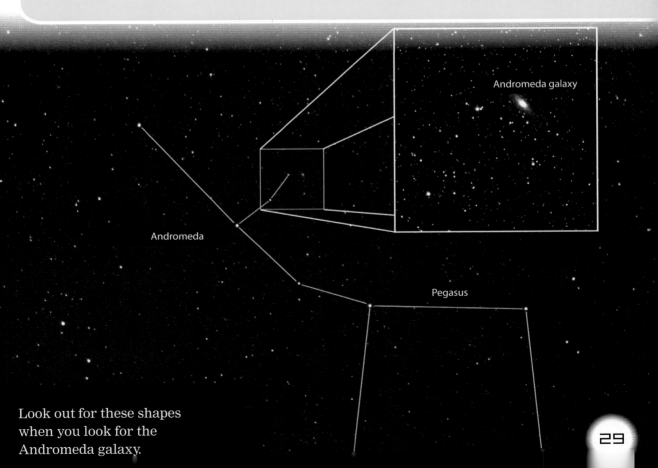

Andromeda galaxy

Andromeda

Pegasus

Look out for these shapes when you look for the Andromeda galaxy.

Other Galaxies

Galaxies can be other shapes besides spirals. Some look like footballs—these are **elliptical galaxies**. Others are lens-shaped (lenticular galaxies). Finally, many smaller galaxies are irregular, meaning they have no clear shape at all.

Elliptical galaxies

Elliptical galaxies range in size from small to very large. One of the best known is the huge galaxy Virgo A, which is about 60 million light-years from Earth. Virgo A has about twenty times as many stars as our galaxy.

Elliptical galaxies usually shine with a reddish light, because they contain mostly older, cooler stars. There are very few gas clouds in these galaxies. All the stars in them seem to have formed at about the same time, with very little gas remaining for new stars to form.

Lenticular galaxies seem to be more similar to flattened elliptical galaxies than to spiral galaxies. They also shine with a reddish light and are made up mostly of old stars.

The Magellanic Clouds are two fuzzy patches of light that can be seen in southern skies. They are small, irregular galaxies that are close neighbors to the Milky Way.

This is Virgo A, the largest of a large cluster of galaxies (see pages 32–33).

Barred spiral galaxies have a central bar rather than a circular hub and two trailing spiral arms. Barred spiral galaxies have more blue stars than other kinds of spiral galaxies.

Spiral galaxies

Spiral galaxies look more varied than elliptical ones. Some have a whirlpool shape, some are side-on discs, and others are in between. The shape we see depends on whether the galaxy is side-on or face-on to Earth, or somewhere in between.

All spiral galaxies have a central bulge and several trailing spiral arms. The central bulge is made up mostly of older stars and has a reddish color. The arms are bluer, because this is where new, hot stars are forming. Spiral galaxies have many more gas clouds than elliptical galaxies, so new stars are forming all the time.

Clustering Together

Galaxies are not spread evenly throughout the universe—they are gathered together in clusters. Some galaxies are part of huge clusters of many thousands of galaxies. Others are in much smaller groups.

Galaxy clusters

Galaxy clusters have hundreds or thousands of galaxies in them. The galaxies in the cluster are held together by gravity. The stars and galaxies that we can see are only a small part of the material in the cluster. The space between the galaxies is filled with gas that is invisible to our eyes. This gas makes up much more of the mass of the cluster than the visible stars.

When stars form, the gas that they form from heats up as it compresses (see pages 14–15). In a galaxy cluster, gravity compresses the gas surrounding the galaxies, and it heats up, too. The gas can reach temperatures of 180 million °F (100 million °C), which is hotter than the center of the Sun!

Smaller groups

Our galaxy and the Andromeda galaxy are part of a small group of galaxies known as the Local Group. Spiral galaxies are most often found in small groups like this. The spiral galaxy shape does not seem to survive in large galaxy groups.

Astronomers can see the gas around a galaxy cluster if they use an X-ray telescope. The picture on the left shows the Coma cluster as seen with a normal telescope. The picture on the right is the same cluster seen through an X-ray telescope.

Colliding galaxies

Gravity pulls the galaxies within a cluster or group toward each other. Sometimes two galaxies crash into each other. When galaxies first collide, they form all kinds of irregular shapes. Yet eventually (after millions of years), the two galaxies join together to form an elliptical galaxy.

Hot News:
Galactic collision

The Andromeda galaxy is on a collision course with the Milky Way. The two galaxies are moving toward each other at a speed of 310,000 mph (500,000 km/h). In about three billion years, the two galaxies will meet and perhaps merge into one huge elliptical galaxy.

This galactic collision is happening in the constellation Canis Major. This could be the Milky Way and the Andromeda galaxy in three billion years.

Quasars and Red Shift

The word *quasar* stands for "quasi-stellar object," meaning something that looks like a star, but is not one. Through a telescope, quasars look like stars, but in fact they are unbelievably bright galaxies. They look like stars because they are very, very far away.

The brightest lights

Quasars shine more brightly than any other objects in the universe. An "average" quasar is over 1,000 times brighter than the Milky Way galaxy, and some quasars are much brighter than this.

Although quasars are incredibly bright, from Earth they look like very faint stars. You need a fairly good telescope to see even the brightest quasar. This is because quasars are extremely far away. The closest quasars are a billion light-years away, and some quasars are over ten billion light-years away. This means that they were shining before Earth and the Sun existed!

Quasars were first discovered using radio telescopes. This image is a radio wave "picture" of a quasar. The long tail is a jet of energy shooting out from the quasar.

The power of black holes

Astronomers think that quasars are galaxies with massive black holes at the center. The difference between a quasar and an ordinary galaxy is that the black hole in a quasar is surrounded by huge amounts of gas and dust. The black hole "eats" this material at an incredible rate. Huge amounts of energy pour out as the gas and dust is "swallowed" by the black hole.

A black hole swallowing material at the rate of a quasar cannot go on forever. Eventually, the center of the quasar stops producing so much energy, and the quasar becomes an ordinary galaxy.

This is a picture of what a quasar might look like close up. The black hole is surrounded by a disc of incredibly hot gases. Jets of energy shoot out from the quasar's center.

HOW IT WORKS:

Active galaxies

Quasars are one example of objects called active galaxies. These are galaxies that have a small central part that produces huge amounts of light and other energy—more than all the stars in the rest of the galaxy. Astronomers believe that the black hole at the center of all active galaxies is surrounded by material that is being sucked in, and that this produces energy. When the material runs out, they will become ordinary galaxies.

Red Shift

When astronomers first looked at quasars, they thought they were stars. But the light from them was not like the light from other stars. In 1963 the German astronomer Maarten Schmidt noticed that the light was similar to light from other stars, but redder. What did this mean?

Zooming away

In fact, "red shifts" had been seen before. In 1929 the U.S. astronomer Edwin Hubble noticed that the light from distant galaxies was redder than expected. The farther away a galaxy was, the redder the light was.

Hubble suggested that the red shift was caused by something called the Doppler effect (see the box on page 37). This meant that the galaxies are moving away from us. The farther away galaxies are, the faster they are moving. However, in quasars, the red shift is greater than for any galaxy. So, according to Schmidt, they cannot be stars. They must be very bright galaxies, farther away from us, and moving away faster, than other galaxies.

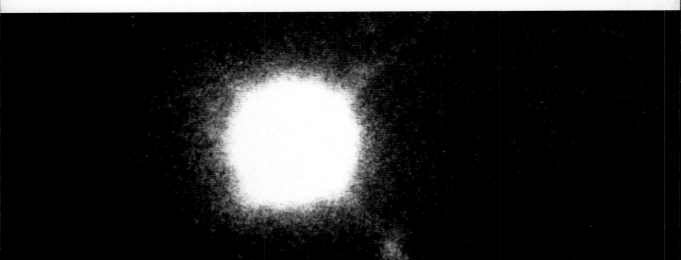

Expanding universe

So, why is everything moving away from Earth? Hubble suggested that it isn't that the galaxies are moving away, but that the whole universe is expanding! You can visualize this by imagining that the universe is a balloon and the galaxies are spots on it. As you blow up the balloon, the material stretches and the spots all move farther apart.

HOW IT WORKS:
Doppler shifts

Imagine you are walking down the street and a police car rushes toward you, siren wailing. As the car goes past, the sound changes. The notes of the siren sound lower. This change in the sound is called the Doppler effect. The siren sounds higher as it comes toward you and lower as it goes away. If something is moving fast enough, the Doppler effect changes the light from it, too. If it is moving toward you, the colors become bluer. If it is moving away, the colors are redder.

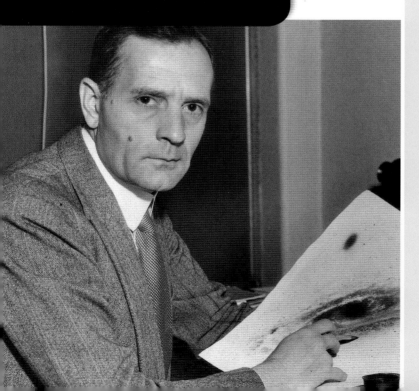

Edwin Hubble was the first person to suggest that the universe might be expanding.

Biography:
Edwin Hubble (1889–1953)

Edwin Hubble was good at many different things. He studied math and astronomy in college, but for a time he worked as a lawyer, and he was also good at boxing. Eventually he became an astronomer at Mount Wilson Observatory, in Pasadena, California. He was the first person to prove that some of the nebulas in the sky were separate galaxies far beyond the Milky Way. He studied many of these galaxies and was the first person to classify (group) them according to their shape.

Rewinding the Tape

If the universe is expanding, this suggests that the universe had a beginning, and that in the past it was smaller than it is today. If we go back in time far enough, we will come to the point when the universe began.

Starting with a bang

Astronomers now think that the universe began suddenly, in an incredible event that they call the Big Bang. Everything in the universe—space, time, and matter (the "stuff" the universe is made of)—appeared in a single moment. The evidence suggests that this happened about fifteen billion years ago.

When the universe first formed, it was very tiny and unimaginably hot. Then, an instant after it formed, it expanded very rapidly and cooled down—at least as compared to how hot it was before. In fact, the temperature was still millions of billions of degrees Fahrenheit! Over the billions of years since then, the universe has continued expanding and cooling.

We tend to think of the Big Bang as an enormous explosion. Before the Big Bang, there was nothing to explode!

Galaxies form

For a very short time, the universe was made up of little but pure energy. A second or so after the universe began, matter began to form. Most of this was made up of the gases hydrogen and helium. Even today, these are the most common substances in the universe.

After a billion years or so, gravity began to pull the clouds of hydrogen and helium into clumps. Stars formed in these clumps and groups of stars joined together to become galaxies. Soon, nearly all the galaxies in the universe were formed.

HOW IT WORKS:
Echoes of the Big Bang

In every direction in space, there is a very small amount of background **radiation** that does not come from stars or galaxies. About 100,000 years after the Big Bang, the whole of space was so hot that it glowed. The universe was opaque (you could not see through it). The background radiation is a faint echo of the burning hot glow of space from before there were stars and galaxies.

This map made by the *Cosmic Background Explorer* (*COBE*) satellite shows the background radiation for the whole of space. The pink areas are slightly warmer and the blue areas are cooler.

Dark Matter

Although astronomers know a lot about the universe and its history, there are still many puzzles they do not understand. One of the biggest puzzles is this: by observing galaxies and clusters, astronomers can get a rough estimate of their mass. The combined gravity of this mass (the stars, gas, dust, and other material) is what holds the galaxy or cluster together. But the sums don't work. There just isn't enough mass. Galaxies and clusters should just fly apart, because gravity is not strong enough to hold them together.

Not enough stuff

Scientists estimate that the universe we can see is less than one-tenth of the total mass. Ninety percent of the mass is missing! There must be more "stuff" somewhere. But where is it? Scientists think that there must be large amounts of matter that we cannot see or detect with any of our telescopes and instruments. They call this undetectable material **dark matter**.

One possible source of dark matter is brown dwarf stars. In 1994 astronomers at the Palomar Observatory, near San Diego, California, took the first ever photo of a brown dwarf. The picture shows a normal star (on the left) with a brown dwarf (center) next to it.

What is dark matter?

Astronomers and physicists disagree about what the missing dark matter might be. Astronomers believe that it could simply be massive objects that do not give out light—for instance, large planets, brown dwarfs (stars that are not large enough to shine), or black holes. So far, nowhere near enough of this kind of matter has been found.

Physicists think that the missing dark matter is made up of tiny particles that are smaller than atoms. Two possibilities are WIMPs and neutrinos. WIMPs stands for "weakly interacting massive particles." They are fairly big (compared to neutrinos) but hardly ever affected by normal material, so we don't know they are there. Neutrinos are very tiny. In fact, they are thousands of times smaller than **electrons**. However, if there were enough of them, they could account for the missing dark matter. The main problem with WIMPs and neutrinos is that, so far, scientists have detected very few of them.

SCIENCE FACT OR SCIENCE FICTION: A world of WIMPs?

According to physicists, WIMPs hardly notice the stuff that we are made of at all. They can pass through solid rock as easily as we can move through air. And we cannot detect WIMPs, either. Who knows? If we learn how to detect WIMPs, we might find that the universe is full of WIMP stars with WIMP planets circling around them and WIMP people living on the planets.

Detecting neutrinos is extremely difficult. This neutrino detector is in a deep mine in the mountains of Japan. The rocks stop any other particles except neutrinos from reaching the detector.

What Next?

We have traveled from the nearest stars to the very edges of the night sky. At the farthest limits, we have found an echo of the beginning of everything: the start of the universe.

But what happens next? The universe has been around for nearly fourteen billion years, and it is likely to be around for a long time to come. But what will happen in the end?

Always expanding

From what scientists know at the moment, it is most likely that the universe will keep expanding, on and on, forever. Eventually, after hundreds of billions of years, all the stars will burn themselves out, and there will be no gas clouds left that can form new stars. The universe will be dead, and there will be nothing left but cold and darkness.

Modern telescopes can look back almost to the start of the universe. But no telescope yet built can look into the future of the universe.

A Big Crunch?

If the scientists have their figures wrong, and the universe is heavier than we think at the moment, then the universe could end in a different way. Some scientists think that eventually the universe will stop expanding. Then, slowly, it will begin to shrink again. As all the stars and galaxies rush toward each other again, space will become smaller and smaller and get hotter and hotter. Eventually everything will come to an end in the opposite of the Big Bang: the Big Crunch. After that, who knows? Some scientists think that as one universe ends, a new one will begin and start expanding all over again.

We will probably never know what will happen to the universe. But one thing is certain: we won't be around when it happens!

Most scientists think the universe will keep on explanding forever. Yet, just possibly, it will shrink again and end in a Big Crunch.

Timeline of the Universe

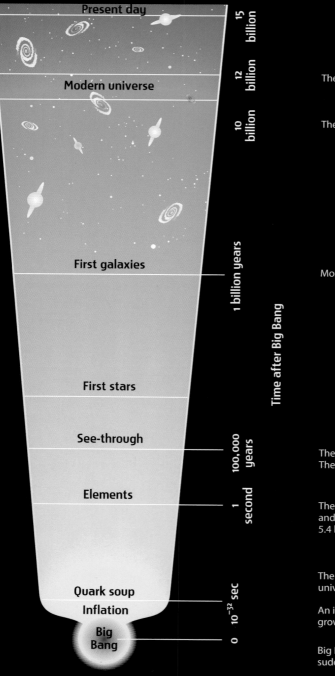

Present day

15 billion

Modern universe

12 billion

The first life on Earth.

10 billion

The Sun forms.

First galaxies

1 billion years

Most galaxies form.

Time after Big Bang

First stars

See-through

100,000 years

The temperature cools to about 4,982 °F (2,750 °C). The universe becomes transparent (see-through).

Elements

1 second

The first elements form, mostly the gases hydrogen and helium. The temperature has dropped to just 5.4 billion °F (3 billion °C).

Quark soup

10^{-32} sec

The first particles of matter appear. Before this, the universe was only energy.

Inflation

An instant after it appears, the universe begins to grow incredibly quickly (inflation) and to cool slightly.

0

Big Bang

Big Bang: An incredibly hot, incredibly tiny universe suddenly appears.

The Ten Brightest Stars

This table shows the ten stars that look the brightest to us. Sirius looks brightest because it is fairly close to Earth. Some of the stars that appear less bright are actually much brighter, but are farther from Earth.

Number	Name	Constellation	Actual brightness*	Distance from Earth (light-years)
1	Sirius	Canis Major	26	8.7
2	Canopus	Carina	200,000	1,200
3	Proxima Centauri	Centaurus	1.7	4.3
4	Arcturus	Boötis	115	36
5	Vega	Lyra	52	25
6	Capella	Auriga	90 70	43
7	Rigel	Orion	60,000	900
8	Procyon	Canis Minor	7	11.4
9	Achernar	Eridanus	400	85
10	Betelgeuse	Orion	15,000	310

*Number of times brighter than the Sun.
Estimates of the distances to stars vary a lot in different sources.
These figures are from the NRAO (National Radio Astronomy Observatory).

Glossary

astrology telling the future from the stars

atmosphere layer of air that surrounds Earth

atoms tiny particles that everything is made of

axis imaginary line through Earth's North and South poles

black hole very tiny, very dense object that has such strong gravity that not even light can escape from it

constellation pattern of stars in the night sky

dark matter matter that scientists believe must exist, but that they cannot detect

dense heavy for its size

electrons very tiny parts of atoms that are electrically charged

elliptical galaxy galaxy shaped like a football

event horizon area around a black hole from which no light can escape

galaxy "island" in space of millions or billions of stars

gravity force between all objects that attracts them toward each other

hydrogen lightest gas, and the main material that stars are made of

light-year distance light travels in one year—about 6 trillion (million million) miles (10 trillion kilometers)

mass amount of matter ("stuff") that something is made of

matter "stuff" that everything in the universe is made of

Milky Way our galaxy, which Earth and the Sun are part of

nebula cloud of gas and dust

neutron star small, very dense lump of material left after a star has exploded in a supernova

nuclear fusion process by which stars make their energy, in which atoms of hydrogen fuse (join) to make helium atoms

nuclear reaction reaction that involves changes to the nucleus (center of an atom)

orbit to go around

quasar originally stood for "quesar-stellar radio source." Now, it refers to "quasi-stellar object," meaning something that looks like a star but is not one.

radiation energy that is transmitted as rays or waves

radio telescope telescope that picks up radio waves from space

red dwarf any star that is about one-tenth the size of our Sun and burns with a cool, reddish light

supergiant very large star, up to several thousand times bigger than the Sun

supernova huge explosion that happens when a very large star reaches the end of its life

universe whole of space, and everything in it

white dwarf small, dense object formed when a small to medium-sized star dies

Further Information

Books

Asimov, Isaac, and Richard Hantula. *Black Holes, Pulsars, and Quasars*. Milwaukee: Gareth Stevens, 2005.

Couper, Heather, and Nigel Henbest. *Black Holes*. New York: Dorling Kindersley, 1996.

Graun, Ken, and Suzanne Maly. *Our Galaxy and the Universe*. Tucson, Ariz.: Ken Press, 2002.

Kerrod, Robin. *The Stars and Galaxies*. Chicago: Raintree, 2002.

Vogt, Gregory. *The Milky Way and Other Galaxies*. Chicago: Raintree, 2001.

Places to visit

Palomar Observatory
35899 Canfield Road
Palomar Mountain, Calif. 92060-0200
phone: (760) 742-2119

Mount Wilson Observatory
740 Holladay Road
Pasadena, Calif. 91106
phone: (626) 793-3100

Websites

Space and Beyond *http://kids.msfc.nasa.gov/Space/*
A website from NASA (the National Aeronautics and Space Administration) about stars, black holes, quasars, and other space stuff. This site also includes the Astronomy Picture of the Day. Every day, this features an incredible picture from space and an explanation of what it is and who took the picture. There is an archive of pictures going back to 1995 and an index organized by subject.

Index